The Blueprint of Oneness

The Blueprint of Oneness

Saint Germain
&
Ashamarae McNamara

FINDHORN PRESS

First published in Great Britain in 2008
by Awakening From Within Ltd

This second edition published by Findhorn Press in 2010
ISBN 978-1-84409-198-0

A CIP Catalogue of this book is available from
the British Library

Cover artwork courtesy of Sheila Clissold
Printed in the European Union

Published by
Findhorn Press
305a The Park, Findhorn
Forres IV36 3 TE, Scotland, UK
t +44(0)1309 690582
f +44(0)131 777 2711
e info@findhornpress.com
www.findhornpress.com

The Blueprint of Oneness

That which I AM has placed the unlocking code within these words and sounds. Together we are unlocking and transmuting those beliefs that have bound your beautiful awareness and veiled your vision of truth that is within you.

—Keeper of the Flame
Ascended Master Saint Germain

Foreword

I have been a channel for spirit for most of my life and, for the past eight years, have been blessed in working with Ascended Masters and other benevolent spirit guides. Sitting working one day with my dear friend Rama, spirit came through and announced that humanity was to be graced with, and we were to deliver, a body of work called *The Blueprint of Oneness*.

Although I could feel its essence, I had no idea what it fully meant. However, I was moved and had a feeling of something astonishing awakening within me – a big "Yes!" feeling is the only way I can describe it. From that point on information came to us – yet only in waves, certainly not all at once. Only when we were ready to receive the next wave about *The Blueprint of Oneness*, would it arrive.

What was, and still is remarkable about this body of work, is that it does not involve adding another story for the mind to play with. It is about direct experience and the transference of energy to support anyone to awaken to the Truth within them.

We have been on an amazing journey with this work since it began. Events, situations and people have come into place in miraculous ways to bring it into existence. I am truly grateful for the wonderful experience this has already been.

You are becoming more than the sum of your parts.
It is your time to wake up!

Blueprint | bloō print|noun a design plan or other technical drawing.• figurative something that acts as a plan, model, or template:

How wonderful would it be to drop unsupportive belief systems effortlessly?

How incredible would it be if we all responded automatically from Grace, Ease, Flow and Love?

How do you feel your life would be if you expressed yourself from that perspective?

Master Saint Germain has said that our natural form of expression is Grace, Ease, Flow and Love. This work is for **you**. Without a doubt you have been calling forth extra ordinary support. This work has been with me a short time and has already blessed my life immeasurably.

May *The Blueprint of Oneness* find its way into your family and friends' hands, and may Grace, Ease, Flow and Love be a predominant experience in your life.

Heart to heart blessings to you and your journey,

– Ashamarae

Believe you are free and that which is outside of you will mould itself to that belief.

Luminous Light

Greetings and welcome to this very auspicious moment. Let us first explain that this body of work is to be experienced through direct inner experience and not read through and through. We recommend that you follow the guidance throughout this work. There will be moments when we will suggest you stop, breathe, feel and allow the energy to move through you.

These recommendations come at the perfect moment for the full integration of the energy being offered to you. What is in your hands is living, yet our statement that this is living will not suffice. Hence we will guide you to and through direct experiences. That way you may know that living energy for self-transformation sits in your hands.

Beloved friend, let me introduce myself — I AM that which is called Saint Germain. I AM that which is called Keeper of the Flame. My purpose in this moment in time is the evolution of humanity and the transition of the Earth Mother into the realms upon which the sublime creations and splendours of light are made manifest. It is truly a rich time for all. Beloved one, it is with great honour that I AM coming to you and that you are reading these words. Many in this world have created interpretations of that which is Saint Germain. So many have laid claim to that which I AM. Beloved, my voice has found itself manifest through many, my communications have been true and real. Yet that which I AM has been placed in a box by so many and it is time to reveal the fullness of that voice which has been made manifest. Do you not see I AM your inner Divine self, I AM your inner call to serve, I AM your inner support in challenging times? Do you not see we are one? Why such an attachment to the form called Saint Germain? At the will of a gentle breath I may manifest and be that which is Saint Germain, for it is a creation by my own hand. Yet I AM so much more.

That which was manifest, that which was called Saint Germain exists within the halls of time, and that which is called Saint Germain speaks now. Many have asked why the name has held such an allure on the mind of the aspirant. Yes, my beloved, the name and title that goes with Saint Germain still exists and serves, yet I AM much more than mere titles.

I AM beyond words, I AM made manifest for

the service and blessings of all humanity, the endless cosmos and the inhabitants that blanket these cosmos. I AM connecting in this moment from the un-real, for that which all believe to be real is but un-real. I am connecting in this moment in a way that has been made manifest from that which is the flame of Christ.

Realize yet again, that which you search for is not outside of you.

The Time Is Now

These words are made flesh that you may ingest them into your bodies and transform your reality into that which is real and upon you in these times of tremendous transition. Beloved daughter, beloved son of the One Source, hear and feel that which communes with you now.

I AM continuing to use this embodied tool called Saint Germain in service to your calling to awaken from the dream of separation. Allow me the honour to grace you with an awakening that will expand your awareness to a reality beyond the words you are reading.

In each letter we have infused an energetic frequency, a truth that will serve you on your path to self-realization. Are you willing to expand beyond your current point of awareness? Are you willing to lay down your wisdom for the truth of the ages that is within you?

I AM sharing with you a truth that is not given

to you, yet is birthed through you. It is truth that will liberate your soul into the realization the sages have spoken so many millennia ago and speak of this day. Will you surrender to the call within you that beckons you to lay your sword down?

Will you release yourself enough to receive the grace that is filling you this moment? Beloved, breathe and feel these words:

It is your time! It is your era! And it is your gift from you, to you! Do you not see this? You have been an expression of endless expressions for eons and eons and it is now time to experience the fullness of your handiwork.

What is being shared with you now is my gift to the awakening consciousness that is emerging. Hear me, O soul of eternity. Believe not in any story that is being presented other than the story of Supreme Love made manifest through you. For that which has found expression in this reality, that which has tormented the hearts and souls of so many, is falling. That which is falling has been ordained to fall, for its creator has given it a gestation period of expression and its time is up. This be not a judgment, it be a natural time of de-manifestation. The time of awakened light manifest through form is now upon all; this is also ordained. For you are the way-showers of this era, you are the beings who have chosen to take form and be the fullness of expressed light. You are the ones who will experience Source through your forms. You have been the one to say, "I will come and experience the one through form, I AM made flesh." Such a time has never been seen, it is truly a glorious time to be here. Realize beloved, you are a singular expression of the One Source and you are awakening to the reality that you, and the one you call Source, are the same.

There is nothing dramatic for you to do to manifest this reality. Follow your inner heart; follow the inner calling to be somewhere, to read something or to do something. Would you not agree that you have always been guided from a source that was more than you could understand and yet it led you to the perfect moment for the most wonderful of experiences? Do you not see that the One Source has placed this in your hands?

For those who feel they have not experienced such guidance, they will. For the time of the great awakening is upon you. Krishna is born, Buddha is manifest and Christ speaks to, and through you. There has never been such a time as it is now, and each moment is vital, each moment is bearing gifts. Open up and receive.

*Take care what choices you make,
you are moulding yourself every
moment of your life.*

Unity

Let us speak of the importance of unity. Unity is not only for the enjoyment of coming together to share and express love. Unity is likened to a tool, an alchemical expression designed to remove the very idea of separation. Unity when actively used will unify the divided helix in each one who participates.

Yet this specific expression of a helix has not been born in individuality and will find expression through united community. To activate this aspect, we recommend you come together in love and service with the intent to manifest Heaven on Earth.

Unity births through the full selfless service from one to another. In such a pattern each one comes to a deep realization, a realization that we will not spoil by adding words to it. The experience is far sweeter and will provide your outer awareness with all that is required for the coming times. Hence, come together, pray together, share together and serve together. This is the way to manifest Heaven on Earth. Coming together in service is one of the greatest tools that you have, and it is yours to use if you choose.

Within these words we have encoded light matrices to activate patterns of light within you. Take a deep breath and you will feel it in this moment. Allow the energy to move through you for as long as you feel guided to.

The key to transcending fear is to move deeply into love.

Receive

What will support your process? Coming together with others who choose a way of love, service, kindness and humility. Share what you have been given, for in the sharing it will expand and will prosper itself for all. You need not wait for the perfect situation, for in the waiting you will wait lifetimes. The time is now to come together in unity and harmony. For each one who reads these words we ask you this: are you willing to share what you have? Are you willing to allow us to assist you to awakening? Are you willing to allow grace into your reality? Will you serve with us side by side? Will you serve the masses that love which heals all illusion and awakens the bliss of Source within each one who will receive it?

Within your "Yes" we will begin immediately. Our intention is to add our energy to what you are already doing, to add energy to the creations that come from your heart's calling. For the plans and ideas you have been pondering have come into your awareness as a grace for the benefit of all. In your "Yes" and in your agreeing to allow us to play a part in your creations, we, who come from realms of pure love and unending bliss, will magnify and purify your vision. Remember beloved, our intention has ever remained the same, and that is to assist all in healing the very idea of separation.

Take the next few minutes, close your eyes, breathe and feel our love.

We bring nothing but love.

'I AM' The Door Which No Man Can Shut And It Is Done

For those who feel the hesitation to answer "Yes", worry not. For I AM always with you and the time will come when you will not hesitate to allow grace to move through you. Our offer will stand for eternity.

The door is always open for those who will receive it. There is nothing within existence that can stop this process of awakening. See and feel the truth for I AM the bridge in which you came and in which you will return. This statement I AM is being shared in mass form now. I AM is being spoken about, thought about and experienced by many. This is not mere jest when we say, your salvation exists within you and I AM THAT, I AM is the bridge in which you, as a singular expression, may experience the fullness that is truth. Your life as you call it is about to have even more amazing shifts.

Love is always looking to see how it can serve, pseudo love is always looking to see how it can be served.

Let Us Pray

Beloved Source, Source that is life, we are thankful for the life and love that is given freely to all. We as one heart, one mind, one body, call on that infinite supply of love to shine through all that which stands in the way of its fullness manifest in this and other worlds. Beloved giver of all, we thank thee from the heart of hearts. Come forth to all of humanity and awaken the sleeper from its dregs of illusion, awaken the dormancy that lay dry and give the sweetest water that is of your pure essence. Give that water that gives life to the lifeless, the water that will quench every heart. So be it and so it is.

Hear me! Awaken Divine One and see the way to the one true love, the one true light and the one truth in all in gratitude. I AM THAT, I AM is the sweetness of all and giver of givers. This moment we anchor a ray of light within your energy field. A ray of pure intention: I AM THAT, I AM.

Thank you, thank you, and thank you. In the name of all that which is Truth, I AM Keeper of the

Flame, Ascended Master Saint Germain.

Now let us cleanse the creations that have found way into form reality and let us see what is there that may be transformed into pure expressions of light. In this moment you contain within you beliefs and experiences that have created a scar of pain. In this moment we will heal those scars, we will wash those pains. For it is in Divine Right that you be free of your past. Take a moment and feel our hand and through loving grace it is done.

Now beloved one, is it not obvious that war will not heal the wounds that run deep in the hearts of so many? Is it not obvious that violence in any form will not bear the fruits of joy? Has it not been said so many times in so many ways, "Love is the way."

Know this reader – Love is all that exists, all else is illusion. Love is the only ingredient missing in the healing of all pain. Love be the 7th seal, truth in form. Until love is allowed through free will to consume all of your experience, you will not know truth in its fullness. You may taste it, you may see it take form, yet the only way to become it in manifestation is to let it consume every act, every thought, to be a full expression of love, come what may. Many will say this is not possible and for those we say, not so. For so many have come and are present in your world now who demonstrate this reality of being love in full expression.

You see beloved, it is not difficult, give your full

committed intent to be love in action. Call on Source within you, and offer all your fear and ask with a full heart:

Beloved source of all, 'I AM THAT, I AM'. Take all I have dreamed and transform it into love in action. Take all that I have created and I will create, and transform it into love in action. I surrender to the will of love and the will of love be done.

In this moment, feel the gift that you are. You are free to choose and you have chosen and choose every moment of your life. Choose Love beloved, choose it now and transform. For "time" in this world is running out. Your seers have shared with you, your guides have shared with you, and your Gurus have shared with you. We have all said the primary message: Serve all and love all. Be love in action and allow love to flow. The opportunity is still fresh for full awakening with the collective that is currently here. We recommend that you use this opportunity, for it is yours and in your hands. Through each action that love is allowed to express, and as you choose to be love in action, you bring forth Source in and through you. I AM THAT, I AM is made manifest.

For the next few minutes, close your eyes, sit still and feel.

Relax, slow down,
you will get everything accomplished
through a calm and steady pace.

Love In Action

Your deeds are the speakers of this and all times. Those which you have called Masters have demonstrated love in action. We ask you, why do we care not for praise or blame? Why are we not affected by opinions? For we bathe and be in the fullness of the Love of Source and in that nothing is required, service is natural and everything bears the fruits of sweetness. Love, joy and unending bliss is the reward for your personality when you choose to allow the birth of your true self. Do you not see that all the money, food and any supply are yours now to have and give? Do not be fooled by the voice that speaks of lack in any form, for this is a lie. This will never ring true in the hearts of those who have seen that they are connected to, part of and one with the Source of Love itself. My friends it is your time, it is you who have come from, and are, Love itself. The mission is to manifest Divine Love into form reality through you. As Divine Love magnifies through you and takes form, all those that do not know of Divine Love will become aware of it by your energy field. As people look upon you, as they talk to you they will receive of the Divine Love that is moving through you and know that your personality is not in the way of this natural flow, it moves through with ease.

Close your eyes, breathe and feel the flow of love moving through you.

Love is the eternal spring,
the fountain of youth
and your salvation.

Your Role Is Vital

See how important your role is. Your life is the vehicle in which pure love will take form. You are the vessel in which Divinity will express. Valuable is quite trivial when you realize who you are and the service you have come to render.

We will speak now about those energies that oppose your awakening. Yes, there are energies that have manifested which use their Source-given right to oppose this transformation. Know this beloved, these energies are quite aware that there is no power over Love.

When a human is being Love, nothing other than love can be in that frequency for very long. Hence, when you are allowing your radiant self to shine, when you allow Love to guide all your actions, anything that is opposite of that will de-manifest. When many come together in Love, dense energy is transformed. Hence you have the energy to stop, change and transform all that which is fear and deception, you have this energy right now in this moment.

Breathe that in.

There are tools that exist to assist you to cleanse the emotional, mental and physical bodies and we highly recommend you use them.

In using such tools you assist your form identity to anchor and express more love from within you. Understand beloved, when we speak of anchor we do not speak of above to below, we speak of within to without, un-manifest to manifest, formless to form.

Silence will mirror for you
that which you hide deep inside.
Silence is your greatest guide.

Serving the Heart

Let us speak of your work and how you may contribute to the sweetness that is finding its way into form. Each one on this planet has a duty and that duty is to be true to the inner heart. For the inner heart is the doorway to truth. Within the heart itself exist multiple streams of reality that can, and will, take form if you would only let it. For these gifts will not be forced upon you, these are created realities from the essence of the One. These realities are beyond what you have imagined Heaven to be. Within your inner heart exists every dream that has ever been called forth in prayer, every answer for the well being of all and the key to release these energies.

Every time you allow love to flow and you act upon the callings of love, you release more of The Blueprint of Oneness into form reality. Every time anyone acts in love they are releasing what is already complete within. Every act is you writing on the canvas of physical life. When each person on your planet acts in love, they are changing the very fabric of reality itself. Do you not see that you are the key, and you are the gift? It is you that the ancients prayed for, it is you that eons of civilizations have prayed to come and transform this and other worlds. All that is required is for you to be love in action. Relax, smile, heal through kindness, serve those who are in need, honour your feelings, shine forth your fullness and be all the love that you are, and reality as you know it will transform.

Why wait when you are ready?

Transcending Doubt

Now there may be a voice, a voice that seems to come out of nowhere and this voice speaks of vengeance and crimes that must be punished. This is the voice of deceit, the voice that would place the seed of fear into your mind. We would recommend for you to deny this voice all access to your beautiful self, deny entry to everything but love. What do we mean by deny? To cease to give attention to anything that does not support Love and Truth to flower through you. Love honours what it is you are feeling in every moment, yet does not project or blame, just allows. 'Allowing' implies being with your feelings, and in being with your feelings your true self transforms heaviness into lightness. It changes the momentum of energy from working against you to working for you and from resistance to flow. From that space truth has the foreground to shine forth.

Be fully aware of what you allow in through your attention and be highly aware of the voice that does its best to convince you that there is something wrong with you. Yes, there are adjustments to be made within the character of individuals, yet wrong denotes judgement and judgement is a vehicle for fear. This voice, if listened to, will dull the truth from birthing through you, the truth that says you have the power of Love to heal the world, let alone your personal life. This voice only has power when it is listened to and it only has power when you give it your attention. Its tools are hoarding, judgment, comparison and greed. The voices of love in action are Kindness, Sharing, Support and Unity. Be vigilant Divine One, put all your attention on love in action and you will feel the truth move through you.

Spend time with those
you choose to be like.

Direct Experience

In this moment I AM
inviting you to receive
a blessing,
a gift of sorts.

As my hand extends to you,
all that is asked is for you
to close your eyes,
relax and breathe.

Take the next few minutes
and receive the blessings.

Direct Experience

Now beloved, does that require an explanation? Will words suffice to capture your direct experience in this moment? Know this beloved, what you have just experienced is an essence of your true nature. This is ever available to you, in every moment. The key to open this door within you is not required anymore, for there is no more door to open. Call this energy forth from within you with clear intention and it is done, whenever and wherever you choose.

Now that the frequency is increased and you are more anchored in this moment, we may move into deeper realities and experiences of who you truly are. As I AM conveying this information through my chela, I AM blending the energy of the Ascended Christ with his consciousness. This way, the energy that is being shared through these words will, in turn, find their way into your reality, that which is your personalized life experience. As you read these living words, your Christ light within is activated and given space to express. You need not quit the work you are doing and run to the hills to shine the fullness of who you are. Things may change, yet dramatics are not required for you to be who you are and to shine that forth. The intention here is that you blend this light into your current expression of life. By doing so you will transform the very collective of the world you are living in. Indeed all peoples are living in different realities and if it were our intent to bring each into the caves of light it would be a very unbalanced world. We will together activate the cave from within. This cave of supreme peace has always been within. In delving into that you open the door for others to enter. As each one crosses your path, they will feel the splendour that emanates from your very being and they will wonder what it is you have that they believe they do not. Some will ask, some will only look and some will move away from you.

Remember that you are here for so many reasons and are here to serve those who have lost their way.

Intend your future,
transcend your past,
this is the foreground
for a peaceful life.

Duty

Who do you believe has been sent to guide humanity into the Golden Age? There are billions of souls and each one is calling to be loved, each one is calling to know that there is purpose in this world of experience and ever changing forms. By the very fact that your eyes have fallen on these words, is the testament that it is you who has come.

What does this mean? What must you do to fulfil your duty in the service of humanity? The duty of the day is to use the tools that were placed within you long before you were born into this world, and your tools shine through to the fullest when you are in the moment.

The truth will not change for convenience. Regardless of your previous experiences, regardless of what others say to you and regardless of what your mind says to you, truth is within. Be here, focus on the moment, honour your feelings and allow your gifts to shine forth naturally through that.

When you are in present moment awareness, your gifts that are to be shared with humanity come forth without effort.

Joy shines forth naturally. This "joy" we speak of is not that joy that has been defined in your books. It is the joy that has no opposite, does not fluctuate with change, and is ever the same. You may only access this space in the present moment. Now we realize there is a momentum of energy that is opposite of Love, Ease, Flow and Grace and this energy requires transmuting. This energy has been created through your belief system and is manifested in your personal life experience. Together we will transform that belief system within you, this way you may know and express the truth of your being through your day-to-day life experience.

We fully understand that this statement "the joy that has no opposite" may not make sense to your personal experience. We extend to you an opportunity that has lain dormant for eons of time. What we are proposing to you is this: in this moment you believe yourself to be reading and/or listening to this dialogue and, from your point of view, this would be so. Yet we invite you to see from an entirely new vantage point, one that expands your awareness as you look through new eyes. It matters not if you can understand what is being shared in this moment. It matters not if it makes sense with your personal experience. What is most important is that you agree to allow the energy that is moving through these words to transform you and activate an awareness that you have not yet experienced.

You see beloved, this energy that is flowing in this moment allows for any individual to accelerate their awareness from the state of consciousness that they are currently occupying. Hence, if you feel you know very little then this energy will expand your awareness from that. If you feel yourself to be highly aware, then this will expand your awareness from there. You can see the beauty that is here in this moment. As you experience what is here in this moment, you are transforming and your awareness is expanded. That which I AM has placed the unlocking code within these words and sounds. Together we are unlocking those beliefs that have bound your beautiful awareness and veiled your vision of the truth.

It has been so long that you have been in hiding and believed that you had to be protected from some unforeseen force. It has been ages that you have believed that you are something other than love. Time to wake up.

Direct Experience

Feel in this moment, yes, this exact
moment, for in this moment we are
pouring forth an elixir of sorts.
A remedy to the illusion of
separation, a remedy to seeing
anything as other than your
beautiful self, that you may finally
wake from this dream.

Close your eyes, breathe and feel.

Within the word the quickening begins.
Follow your inner call, for this moment is yours alone, beloved traveller.

The Key Within

Within every experience exists the life force that is your very being. My beloved, you are dancing within your own field of awareness and have ever only been playing a game. This will not fully be accepted by the mind and that is why we have provided the key to activate The Blueprint of Oneness from within you. Oneness does not take away the joy of experiencing people, events or things; it enhances them. For when you are fully aware of the unity that connects all that is, your experience of the world and all that is in it becomes a wonder beyond which your mind has created.

There are those in your history who discovered the key to the code of The Blueprint of Oneness, and when they did they immediately surrendered to that aspect of themselves and they became what you call enlightened. They birthed nirvana in the "now" moment they were experiencing.

The key may manifest in various forms. One may receive it through the blessings of a master, one may activate it through a tragedy and one may spend lifetimes in spiritual practice.

For within the service to Source, we of the Ascended Masters sent forth a prayer from the depths of our being, on behalf of our beloved brothers and sisters who are lost in illusion. A prayer that contained no words was offered to lift humanity out of self-destruction and give every possible tool and opportunity to rebirth truth from within each one. It was ordained by that which you call Source, that this energy be released to the masses for the blessings of love itself. That love is YOU. This is one of those gifts, one of those blessings and it sits in your hands now. Within this energy is a gift from the luminous heart of those who be and express only love in service to all. We have awakened to truth, we are experiencing the wonder that is beyond description and this reality is at hand for your universe.

Join us in this moment and feel the energy moving through your embodiment. Close your eyes, breathe and feel.

Remember, in the palm of your hands
sits the energy of the universe.

Activation

This is only the beginning, beloved. As each one connects with The Blueprint of Oneness, their very presence transforms everything around them. Unity is made manifest, and within that unity Love, Ease, Flow and Grace flowers through you. Love is the closest word that points to who you truly are. Ease and Flow are your natural way of creating, and Grace is what moves through your life expression.

Before it was chosen to create worlds of form, the one Source placed within each and every Source-free being the key home. This home is not a place that one goes to. It is a state of being, being that which you truly are, being that which has no opposite. As you are ingesting this energy, you are experiencing yourself as a separate part from the whole. You have a name, you have some form of title and you are choosing to express yourself in a specific way. Yet underneath all of that is the Oneness that is life itself.

That which gives life, that which is behind the

name and form is Truth, the one reality. The key that sits within you in this moment is the key that unlocks your belief system from the limits you have allowed to enter your sublime self. Source knew that within the dance of form, the child, the one expression, would forget and would get lost within itself. Source knew that for the child to find its true self, it would create form after form in search of the father. Hence, Source placed Source within the child and that is the key; Source is the key and Source is now. Jesus and Mary activated this Blueprint of Oneness from within, Moses did, Buddha did, and now you are. How will this affect your life? Let us make this simple for you to understand. You have a body, a specific life expression, a path and a gift to bring forth to this world. This activation will assist every form, every act, every experience you are creating to become more of the beauty that you are, which is truth within your very being.

All the wonder you have ever beheld
is an expression of your beautiful self.

I AM THAT, I AM

It has been shared with all of humanity time and time again. Source is one with its creation. Your form, life experience, your friends, everything you can see and feel is Source. There is no place for you to go to experience Source. Source is active through the "you" personality. Source has ordained for you to awaken to truth within. You are not separate or different from Source. All that stands in the way of this is your belief that you are separate. In this gift from Source you can transmute and transform those beliefs that bind you from awakening. Within this awakening Source manifests through your very experience and life takes on a whole new meaning. Source is at hand beloved. Source or God or Goddess, as they have been used, are far from the written words in your holy books. For when one seeks to define that which is Source, in that moment the truth that is Source is lost. We will not look to define that which you will experience directly. Direct experience is what is being offered here to you. This way there will be no room left for uncertainty. You will know in a way that is perfect for you and is beyond the mind's way of knowing. It will pulsate through you, it will shine through your eyes and you will see in a whole new way. Remember, Source knows your heart's desire, Source knows what you truly long for and Source has ordained that you awaken from the dream. In that awakening you will naturally bless everything with the light of Love in action. I AM THAT, I AM.

Repeat this in your mind now and feel. For we will add the fires of our love in this moment as you repeat the following: I AM THAT, I AM as many times until you feel complete.

So it is and so be it.

You are being baptized by the all-consuming flame. Let the flame consume you.

Supporting The Process

There are seven specific actions we recommend for you to focus on to support the anchoring of The Blueprint of Oneness into your personal life:

1 Giving

It has been said countless times, it has been proven over and over, give and ye shall receive. There is none other than you, if you are unwilling to give to yourself, you automatically cannot receive from yourself. You have so much. Give a smile, give a hug, acknowledge beauty, support those who have less: give, give, give. Beloved, it is not about what you give. It is all about how you give. Giving because you think it is the right thing to do is still missing the essence of who you are. We recommend you give for the sake of love itself and fill every act of giving with love and giving for the joy of it. So many hearts are calling to be loved, so many have forgotten that they are one with all that is. It is love in action that fills the gap, transforms a life and awakens the sleeper. Begin now and experience the beauty and grace that comes from being love in action. Do not take our word for it: test it, see and experience for yourself.

2 *Receiving*

When you are in flow you become aware of the ease of life. This flow births itself through the love that is one with all of creation and that is available to you now in this moment. When you are giving to others, you are honouring the beauty of all that is. Then, you automatically receive the energy inherent in those acts. This energy comes through feelings and when you experience those feelings that enliven the body with the sensation of joy, in that moment allow it to move through you completely. That energy that is moving through your embodiment is highly magnetic and brings to you whatever is required for you to experience oneness, joy and abundance in all ways. What supports your life will just arrive out of the blue and you will see that you never had to put effort into anything to experience a rich life. All that was required for the riches of Source was to give the love of Source and experience Source while in the body. The access point for this is the now, this moment, hence the door is open. Welcome...

3 *Gratitude*

It is quite simple. As you are grateful for all that you experience, you become aware in that moment of the Oneness that is. Gratitude opens the floodgates to direct experience of unending joy and unity. As you acknowledge every form and every experience as that which is a part of who you are, separation loses its grip. Gratitude is a far greater tool than most realize and when used on a consistent basis, life's wonders reveal themselves and joy becomes a constant companion.

4 *Breathing*

Breath is the window into the silence that pervades all that is. Beloved, you are breathing anyway and you are using this tool all the time. Yet we offer you the opportunity to breathe with conscious awareness. Simply witness the breath and give it some attention while you do what you do. The mind will argue that you cannot function in life productively and be focused on your breath at the same time. This is far from the truth. As you practice the art of conscious breathing, your awareness of energy and various frequencies that are moving around and through you increases.

Your ability to act in a more fluid and graceful

way happens easily and without effort. Again, test it and see for yourself.

5 *Relaxation*

This is vital to anchoring Oneness through your form experience. Being relaxed has nothing to do with non-action and everything to do with action. The body and mind relax the more you are focused on what it is you are doing, hence being present. One can experience a challenging situation and still be relaxed. The door into relaxation is breath. Breathe and feel the inner energy of your body and you will relax automatically. Do this in your daily life and see what happens.

6 *Allowing*

Non-resistance to what has already occurred is vital. The main tool to allowing is to feel and accept, then allowing comes of its own accord. Allowing opens you to feeling the Oneness of all that is and brings your awareness to the reality within. Allowing never implies that you choose not to change a situation. It fully implies that you are empowering yourself to receive the fullness of the gift that is being offered in the moment of any experience, and from that space your choices to change the situation through Ease and Grace are vast. Within any experience there is tremendous opportunity and when you connect to that unity of Oneness within yourself, that which is outside of you changes. Why? Oneness responds to Oneness, Love responds to Love, whether the outer experience is aware of the change or not. When you are coming from a united viewpoint, the whole of the universe rushes in with full momentum to transform the illusion of separation back into Oneness.

7 I Am That, I Am

Oneness activated through unity is made manifest: I AM THAT, I AM. The essence of One brought into form. Christ consciousness, Buddha nature, I AM THAT, I AM. This statement will bring such blessings to the one who actively uses it. The key here is to use this for the blessings of all and the transformation of your world. Within I AM THAT, I AM is the fullness of who you are and is the vehicle for which that expression takes form. Chanting I AM THAT, I AM, with the intent of manifesting unity through the Oneness of all being, will bring tremendous benefit to all Creation.

Now as you begin to utilize these tools within your daily life, there will be a wonderful transformation that will provide you with all that is required for your Heaven on Earth. The intention here is that you merge this light into your current expression of life. By doing so you will transform the very collective of the world you are living in. We will together activate the cave within. This "cave" as we are calling it is a metaphor for your true home. Home is a metaphor for your true state of being.

This cave of Supreme Peace has always been there for you. In delving into this space, you open this door for others to enter. We say again, as each one crosses your path they will feel the splendour that emanates from your very being and they will wonder what it is you have that they believe they do not. Some will ask you, some will only look and some will run from you. Remember that you are here for many reasons, and you are here for those who have lost their way. Who do you believe the Divine Principle has sent to guide humanity into the Golden Age? There are billions of souls and each one is calling to know that there is purpose in this world of experience and ever-changing forms. By the very fact that your eyes have fallen on these words is the testament that it is you who has come.

We are working together for the greater good of all of humanity and it is the intent of those who dwell within luminous light to call your attention to the great awakening within you. It need not be dramatic: indeed it is more like a handshake, a hug or a smile. It is quite simple really. I AM offering you in this moment to take my hand in friendship and service to all. In this handshake as we are calling it, is the agreement to receive the light of love from the ascended heart and to allow it to touch every area of your life.

In that movement of light we will accelerate your ability to give from your sacred heart. This is not a mere jest, for we have foreseen this moment in time. We have agreed to play our part in this drama called the Awakening of Consciousness within form reality.

You have agreed to play your role and together as one, in service, the mission will be done.

Direct Experience

We will begin an activation
of light in this moment.

Take the next few minutes,
close your eyes, breathe
and feel the energy that is
moving through.

Your are an embodiment of pure love and light. Remember, it takes more energy to play victim than to play free.

Manifest

Each one on the planet is manifesting in their own way. As you manifest through the vehicle of clear intent, the natural occurrence of Love, Grace, Ease and Flow will become prevalent in your life. As you allow the release of control, struggle ceases its hold and you will grasp the real truth of manifesting.

There is a formula in the world of form to manifest and you use it daily and most of the time unconsciously. Yet there is another way to manifest that is far simpler and that is to let go and let Source within you. There has not been one on this planet who did not have the secret of manifestation, who in a moment did not release beauty in the form of smile, laughter and/or gratitude to the Source it was drawing from. Yet as you go to create and manifest your abundance, you have become so serious, and seriousness is heaviness. It is this heaviness that weighs down your creation, that which you choose to experience.

Let go and let Source within you guide your way. A key is to be present and bathe in the silent space within. From that space you will know exactly what to do. Remember the silence within is the guru. There are those who are on the path of awakening, "servants of light", and the majority of them are lacking something to support their path. When you discover the source within, you have only touched the surface in the deepest of oceans. As you merge deeper and deeper into Source, into the silence within, all the forms around you will take care of themselves. Ground yourself within and everything that is required for a fruitful life manifests beautifully. Yet the mind will not validate this. Understand that the mind will not validate truth until it is united with heart.

You see beloved, life is changing and is changing in support of the grand awakening. For you have prayed for peace. You have prayed that life would flow in all ways to support your path. You have prayed for the light of love and have asked for that to manifest in all your experiences. That time is upon you now, in this moment. As each one transforms their own personal life, they will automatically anchor Heaven on Earth. We have scribed, as it is known on Earth, this opportunity being offered to you now.

Enough of humanity have chosen love and that has opened the floodgates of light from deep within. We see an opportunity for those who are willing to anchor a wave of light that has yet not been experienced in such numbers. This wave of light will birth itself from deep within. Allow us to assist in the process of this birth. Consider us as midwives, we will hold your hand, adjust your position and assist in every way for you to have a gentle birth. The Blueprint of Oneness will open the gates of prosperity in ways that are unknown to those who have not experienced the fullness of Source. It is Source alone that manifests, it is Source alone that creates opportunity and it is Source alone that will transform your life.

The Blueprint of Oneness is a grace beyond measure, for that which you choose to create will come from a place that will automatically serve the whole for the greater good of all. From that point of awareness The Blueprint of Oneness draws everything that is required for you to anchor and manifest the sublime creations that are moving through you!

Congratulations.

Thy Will Be Done

Feel this truth beloved. Jesus knew that Source already took care of everything. Source had already ordained the greatest good and from that Jesus allowed everything to just come through him. He resisted nothing, for he saw through the eyes of the One Source and could see the perfection in every act that was laid out before him. Did he have free will? Of course he did, yet he chose Source's will and in choosing Source's will, he awoke Source within him. Thy will be done! This was a gift beyond gifts to humanity. The ego has fooled many into believing that you would become like a slave with "Thy will be done" and in believing that, you have become a slave to the ego. "Thy will be done" is the allowing of Source's grace to transcend your ego into full Source awareness while in form reality. It is a gift that, when used, will transform your actions into all loving actions without the fight or the struggle to do what you know inside will serve the greatest good. You will automatically choose the greatest good for yourself and all of creation when you allow Source to guide your way. You are moving into full Source realization anyway my love. "Thy will be done" is likened to laying down your struggle for total ease and grace active in your life.

Direct Experience

Take the next few minutes,
close your eyes,
breathe and softly repeat
"Source within and without,
Thy will be done."

Now take some time to write
down some words about
your direct experience.

This will support to anchor
the experience within you.

Trust what you feel, for it is Love that speaks through you in this moment.

The Silent Space Within

There is a silent space that exists in this moment and in every moment of your life. It is that silent space that will bring you the knowing and understanding of your confusion. For confusion is the root of doubt, and doubt is the mother of confusion. Yet silence has no question of such a statement. Yet you may observe in this moment how mind instantaneously brings in the information and dissects it to understand, and it is this understanding that you search for which creates your torment. For all of your understandings what has it brought to you? It brought you to a new land of more questions, searching for more understanding to those questions, and it is an endless journey. The one who resides without questions is truly free.

Now let us continue this conversation. Was it not said, "Be like children"? When children are very little they do not care what you think of them, they do not need you to validate who they are. When you, as an adult, validate everybody's point of view of you according to their personal judgments, you give energy to their judgments and you bond them to yourself. Let the silence within you show you who you are. Source within you does not judge.

Source supports you, reveals you and moves through you and provides all that is required for a beautiful life. We ask you this: "Where has your control led you?" It has led you to struggle. For who does not struggle daily in one form or another? There is no need to struggle! What is there to struggle for? Everything is yours already, for everything is energy and energy moves at will with your choice and attention. See this once and for all and life will change in amazing ways. Remember everything that is required for a fruitful life appears with Ease, Flow and Grace when you allow the inner source to guide you.

Indeed this truth was given to the world by those you would call Masters long ago and the same truth is being shared now. One way to increase the flow in your life is humour, so let us talk about this. Humour is one of the greatest gifts that you have and it has the power to heal and clear out the heaviness in your life. There is so much to laugh at and there is so much to celebrate in your world. Is there truly any reason why you have to be so serious about your life? Yes, there are times when you must focus more than other times, this we would agree, yet do you really believe seriousness works for you? Yet when you look for the humour in life, you will most certainly find it and when you allow that humour to move through you, the energy around you shifts in amazing ways. Many people have lost their sense of humour because they still allow husbands, wives, friends, media or other people to validate who they are. Call forth validation from the One Guru within you and let go of the opinions of others. Remember, all guides and gurus in the world are supporting you to connect with your inner source. Let it forth, surrender to that aspect within you and witness the miracle that is life. Feel the vibration of the space around you in this moment and the space within you. As you allow Divine Vibrations to flow, your vibration raises to a frequency beyond separation, hence separation disappears for that moment. Yet realize it wasn't there in the first place; separation is only an idea, it is only a frequency, a wave of energy created out of the mind. As you increase your love vibration, fear does not become so solid in the body.

Within the shortest time man will begin to use the energy of Love as a whole for the entire planet; for total healing, for movement from one place to another and for all the powering requirements that you use on a day-to-day basis. This reality of love being used for everything has been active for thousands of years by Masters in many parts of the world. Yet your minds can only accept the concept of it, for if you broke your leg you would go to the doctor, would you not? You would accept the doctor's castings, yet soon you will mend a break with your vibration, and how will the break mend? It will never happen, for the full awareness and depth of love keeps you safe from so-called accidents. Yet you need not wait years for this, for we have opened the door to accelerated growth and for those who choose to allow the Ascended Masters to support them in the awakening process, it is done. All that is required is that you announce it in this moment. For in this moment we are by your side and it is your YES to our gift that will activate the process.

*It is your nature to create and to be creative.
Breathe, feel, and be the moment
and freedom is yours.*

Practice

Let us speak of practice. What is not practice in this world? It took practice to forget. It took practice to be stubborn and it takes practice to remember who you are. Practice from our point of view is not the same as yours. For practice may be defined as "consistent attention on a given choice for the highest outcome".

You beloved, as you continue to give your attention unto Source within, you draw out that to express through your life. That is what we do in action, it is our only action and this one action takes care of everything in advance. Yet you are free-willed, you have choice and look what your collective choice has created. We are not here to judge you, my love. Yet the truth of your collective creation remains. Your forest which sustains your air, your water which supports your body and your Earth which holds you in her loving embrace is all threatened by greed and fear. There is time to transmute all of this. The Divine, shining through you, is what will transform this world. It will be the energy of Love that will change the planet, it will be the energy of Love that will transform your collective and it will be the energy of Love that will illumine your soul.

Love, as we are speaking of it, is far more than the mind may comprehend. Love that comes from Source within, Love that is not tainted by need and greed is the Love that changes all that which seems impossible to change. Whatever seems to be impossible is possible through the Love of Source within you. Why have the Avatars and Masters not changed the world for you? The reason is because you have the power to do it yourself and it is time to wake up to that truth. You have the same love within you that Jesus had and it is that love which raised the dead and gave life to that which had no life.

We speak truth when we say that we are ready to assist you to awaken to the fullness within. We are bringing together those who have continuously called on Source and asked for the power to create planetary change for the greater good of all. Your prayer is answered and we come bearing gifts. Beloved, you have the energy to bring healing to the souls that suffer, the souls that are lost. You have all that is required within you to support the awakening in the collective of humanity. You who are reading this now, your role is vital and you came as one who would make change in everything you touched. Together, along with thousands of others who will activate The Blueprint of Oneness within the framework of this world, we will create a wave of healing light that has never been seen. Together we will manifest Heaven on Earth and there is nothing in existence that can or will stand in its way, for the way has been made clear.

I AM Saint Germain, I have walked in this world with you, I have talked with you and together we have made plans and those plans are coming to fruition. That which is Saint Germain makes you this promise: "Take my hand and together we will transcend fear in this life. Take my hand and I will walk you to the gates of truth and I will bear witness to the illumination of your soul." For it is my promise that you be awakened and that promise will not be thwarted. Take my hand now and witness the truth manifest through you. In my promise I offer you proof that this is real and true. Within three days time I will create an experience that leaves no room for doubt that I AM with you and that together we are transforming the world for the greater good of all and for the full expression of love manifest.

In this moment I AM embracing you and I AM ever grateful. In the fullness of Love and in the service of the One,

I AM Saint Germain, Keeper of the Flame.

You stand ready,
humanity has been waiting for you,
go forth and shine!

The Blueprint of Oneness:

the audio experience

Any action that is done consistently will create an imprint on the mind and this will form a natural habit to occur.

Ashamarae and Saint Germain have recorded a prayer, a commentary and a meditation designed to liberate you from limiting beliefs and anchor you to your divine self within.

To listen to the meditation (Track 3), we recommend that you use personal headphones and create a space where you will not be disturbed, so as to support the full experience of this meditation.

Tracklisting:

1. Blueprint of Oneness Prayer

2. Blueprint of Oneness Commentary

3. Blueprint of Oneness Meditation

All 3 tracks are available as mp3s for download from:

www.findhornpress.com

Other available audio from Ascended Master Saint Germain

Available as mp3s for download from:

www.findhornpress.com

Awakening from Within

The organization ***Awakening From Within*** has been brought together by Ascended Master Saint Germain. The mission of ***Awakening From Within*** is to be of service and support to Mother Earth and her inhabitants. It is during this pivotal shift in consciousness that we are called to connect and unite with all those who choose love and together shift the current consciousness into one of unity, love and equality for all. We as a team serve hand in hand with the Ascended Masters, various beings of love and other organizations who are also in service to humanity and Mother Earth. Our service is primarily with Master Saint Germain; Master works through each of us in specific ways to support anyone to co-create a direct experience of the love and magnificence within themselves.

For more information, please consult:
www.awakeningfromwithin.com

Acknowledgments

How can I ever thank enough my teachers, friends and guides: Saint Germain, Red Feather and the all-pervading Mother-Father-God-Goddess. Thank you for always being there and blessing my life, I am forever grateful.

To my wife Narayani, I love you. Your many sacrifices helped make this possible. You are one of the most amazing women I have ever met. I thank you and am honoured you are a part of my life.

Thank you to my two sons, Bodhi and Noah. You are amazing teachers for me and your love and presence has assisted me in growing up. I love you.

To my dear friend Rama, without you this work would not be the amazing grace it is. Thank you.

To Shanna, Gema, Helen and Julia your service and dedication have been invaluable. Thank you.

To Sheila, thank you for bringing forth the beautiful artwork that graces this book.

To beloved Ortalia, your teachings and love run deep in me. Thank you for being the magnificent being that you are.